Alive in the WORD

VIRTUES FOR DISCIPLES

PRAYER

Biblical Wisdom for Seeking God

Michelle Francl-Donnay

Little Rock Scripture Study

LITURGICAL PRESS
Collegeville, Minnesota

www.littlerockscripture.org

Nihil obstat: Rev. Robert Harren, J.C.L., *Censor Deputatus.*
Imprimatur: ✠ Most Rev. Donald J. Kettler, J.C.L., D.D., Bishop of St. Cloud, May 7, 2021.

Cover design by Ann Blattner. Cover photo: Getty Images.

Photos/illustrations: Pages 7, 12, 14, 17, 19, 21, 25, 27, 30, 34, 37, 39, 42, 43, Getty Images. Used with permission.

ISBN: 978-0-8146-6405-6; 978-0-8146-6430-8 (e-book)

Contents

Introduction

Alive in the Word brings you resources to deepen your understanding of Scripture, offer meaning for your life today, and help you to pray and act in response to God's word.

Use any volume of **Alive in the Word** in the way best suited to you.

- **For individual learning and reflection**, consider this an invitation to prayerfully journal in response to the questions you find along the way. And be prepared to move from head to heart and then to action.
- **For group learning and reflection,** arrange for three sessions where you will use the material provided as the basis for faith sharing and prayer. You may ask group members to read each chapter in advance and come prepared with questions answered. In this kind of session, plan to be together for about an hour. Or, if your group prefers, read and respond to the questions together without advance preparation. With this approach, it's helpful to plan on spending more time for each group session in order to adequately work through each of the chapters.

- **For a parish-wide event or use within a larger group,** provide each person with a copy of this volume, and allow time during the event for quiet reading, group discussion and prayer, and then a final commitment by each person to some simple action in response to what he or she learned.

This volume on the topic of prayer is one of several volumes that explore **Virtues for Disciples.** Each of us is called to be a disciple, a follower of Christ. The life of a disciple is challenging, but it is the most fulfilling way to live. Called by name by the God who created us, we are shaped by the teachings of Christ and continually guided by the Holy Spirit. As we grow more deeply into this identity as disciples of Jesus Christ, we discover the valuable virtues that mark God's people.

Prologue

At its core, prayer is the act of turning toward God, responding in love to the One who created us. In prayer not only do we call out to God, but God endlessly calls out to us, ever enfolding us in mercy, drawing us close in love.

Why do I pray? You might as well ask me why I breathe. I breathe so I can sing. I breathe to pause. I breathe, awake or asleep, whether I'm aware of it or not. So, too, do I pray. I pray like I breathe, that I might live. Prayer is, as St. John of the Cross said, the "breathing of God in the soul, of the soul in God."[1]

Yet unlike breathing, prayer is something we must learn and—again and again—choose to do. The Scriptures have much to teach us about prayer. The passages and commentary contained in this small book barely touch the surface. My only hope is that these brief reflections will encourage and support those who seek the face of the Lord and long for him (Ps 42:3), those who wish to breathe in Christ.

Of course, it is not enough to read about prayer. We must practice it. And when we are anxious about prayer, worried whether we are "doing it right," pastor and spiritual director Daniel Ruff, SJ, has reassuring advice: "The only way to go wrong in prayer is not to do it at all." All the wisdom of Scripture, saints, and sages can be summed up in a single word of instruction: *pray*.

Thirsting for God

Begin with a few quiet moments, asking God to assist you in your prayer and study. Then read and pray this excerpt from Psalm 63.

Psalm 63:1-9
1 A psalm of David, when he was in the wilderness of Judah.

2 O God, you are my God—
it is you I seek!
For you my body yearns;
for you my soul thirsts,

In a land parched, lifeless,
   and without water.
3I look to you in the sanctuary
   to see your power and glory.
4For your love is better than life;
   my lips shall ever praise you!

5I will bless you as long as I live;
   I will lift up my hands, calling on your name.
6My soul shall be sated as with choice food,
   with joyous lips my mouth shall praise you!
7I think of you upon my bed,
   I remember you through the watches of the
      night
8You indeed are my savior,
   and in the shadow of your wings I shout for joy.
9My soul clings fast to you;
   your right hand upholds me.

Following a brief time of reflection on the psalm, consider the background information provided below in Setting the Scene. The questions in the margins may be used for personal reflection or group discussion.

Setting the Scene

Our first lessons in prayer often come from listening to our parents or grandparents pray. Long before we understand the words, we sense their rhythm, whether the steady beat of the rosary or the familiar rumble of grace before meals.

The book of Psalms is a collection of 150 prayers, offering us lessons in prayer from those who have gone before us in faith. The psalms are ancient. Some have roots going back thousands of years to the Bronze Age. Indeed, our Jewish sisters and brothers have been singing their praises to God in some of these words since before the time of Miriam and Moses. While their composition is traditionally attributed to King David, the psalms were most likely composed by a number of different poets over the centuries and eventually gathered into a single collection.

In the Jewish tradition, the book of Psalms is titled simply "Praises" (*Tehillim* in Hebrew). These "praises" are both prayer and poetry. At their heart they acknowledge God's boundless power and glory in a way that bursts with intensity. God's glory is so immense that we cannot express our praise in words alone and instead are driven to sing! In fact, our English word "psalm" derives from the Greek word for songs that are sung to the music of harps. Collections of psalms are sometimes called "psalters," from the Greek word for the stringed instruments that might accompany their singing.

The *Catechism of the Catholic Church* calls the book of Psalms "a masterwork of prayer" that deserves a permanent place both in the prayer of the church and in our own personal prayer.[1] Of course, like our Jewish brothers and sisters, Christians do pray with the psalms regularly (as Paul exhorted the Ephesians to do; Eph 5:19). We respond to the word of God with a psalm at Mass (the responsorial psalm). In the *Gloria* and at the preparation of the gifts for the Eucharist, our prayers come from the psalms. The psalms also form the backbone of the Liturgy of the Hours, prayed by religious communities, priests, deacons, and many laity.

The images used by the ancient psalmists are often vivid, stripped of pretense. They are grounded in common everyday experiences, from the sticky slime of snails (58:9) to shattered dishes (31:13). Anyone who has shared a bedroom with a mosquito will grasp the frustration of the psalmist cornered by persistent enemies, whom the psalmist compares to a swarm of bees (118:12). The Cistercian monk Thomas Merton called the psalms "rugged and sober."[2] These prayers are "rugged" indeed, refusing to shy away from fraught and difficult situations: illness, death, starvation, war, sin, and rebellion. They show us a way to approach our God who is rock and fortress—unassailable, unbreakable. We can say anything to God and still be cherished sons and daughters.

Yet the psalms are not all sober and serious. They can resound with immoderate joy, celebrating births and marriages, banquets and harvests with wild dancing and blasting horns! The psalms are as much a mirror of our resurrections as they are of our agonies.

What are your earliest recollections of prayer experiences? Who in your life has taught you about prayer or modeled prayer for you?

Psalm 63, an excerpt of which we will examine now, is a psalm of great yearning. With poetry, images, and emotions, the psalmist will help us put words to our own deepest longings.

Psalm 63:1-9 will now be explored a few verses at a time to deepen your understanding of the passage. Reflect on the text and questions along the way.

Understanding the Scene Itself

[1]A psalm of David, when he was in the wilderness of Judah.

Many of the psalms are introduced with a superscription—a line of description or instruction. Sometimes the superscription suggests what instruments should accompany the psalm, such as stringed instruments (4:1) or wind instruments (5:1). At other times the superscription links the psalm with a particular person or biblical event, such as King David's escape from Saul (18:1). Psalm 63 is set in the moment when David has fled to the mountainous region of Judah and is hiding from Saul, in fear of his life (see 1 Sam 23:14-15).

Prayer is often an urgent response to a particular situation in which we find ourselves. We may be in danger or facing temptation, and we ask God to protect and deliver us. Or perhaps we are responding to overwhelming joy as we see a spectacular sunset or hold a newborn child. Yet prayer is more than these spontaneous moments. Prayer is also something we must attend to regularly. The *Catechism of the Catholic Church* suggests that making a habit of praying at specific times and in particular places can prepare us to pray at the moments when we are most in need of God.[3]

When have you found yourself in a "wilderness" or trapped by your own circumstances, reaching out for God?

[2]O God, you are my
God—
it is you I seek!
For you my body yearns;
for you my soul
thirsts,
In a land parched, lifeless,
and without water.

This psalm opens by expressing a need for God that is so immense, so all-encompassing, that it is hard to imagine what could satisfy it. The psalmist isn't expressing a vague preference—say, for coffee rather than tea—but is describing a profound, utterly consuming desire, like that felt by lovers who can't wait for their beloveds to arrive, or by someone in terrible pain who longs for relief. We yearn for God in prayer with a single-minded intensity; nothing else—nothing less—will satisfy us.

But the psalm suggests that this longing is even deeper than we can imagine. It invites us to contemplate a vast countryside spread out before us—dust billowing; dried leaves rustling on the trees; dead, brown grass crunching underfoot; riverbeds bereft of water. It would take unimaginable amounts of water to bring such a landscape to life, more than a million gallons for every acre. In the wilderness where David found himself, it would have taken billions of gallons of water falling from the sky each and every year, soaking into the scorched ground and flooding the plains, to turn such a parched land green, to fill the empty riverbeds. Our souls, implies the psalmist, thirst for God like this sere land thirsts for water—intensely, with a need more desperate than we can envisage or express.

Do you long to encounter God in prayer? How might you describe this longing?

This thirst is not ours alone. Our prayer is rooted not so much in our desire for God but in God's desire for *us*. In reflecting on the encounter between Jesus and the Samaritan woman at the well, St. Augustine points out that Jesus' thirst is not so much for the literal water from the well but rather for the woman's faith in God.[4] On the night of the Last Supper, just before offering the disciples the cup of his blood and the bread that was his body, Jesus expressed this desire: "I have ardently longed to eat this Passover with you" (Luke 22:15, NJB). In the original Greek, the word for "longing" or "desire" is repeated, underscoring how much God thirsts for us.

Are you willing to encounter God's overwhelming love in prayer? What might be stopping you?

Hard as it might be to imagine, God intensely hungers and thirsts for us. Prayer, our intimate dialogue with the Lord, is the intersection of God's thirst with ours.

3I look to you in the sanctuary
to see your power and glory.

In his letters, St. Paul tells us that God is so close to us that we are sanctuaries, dwelling places for the Holy Spirit (2 Cor 6:16; Eph 2:22). In prayer we encounter not some distant and aloof God but a God who is close to us, who shares our flesh, who knows our strengths, our needs, and our thirsting. But we also recognize that God is far beyond what we can grasp. In this verse, the psalmist reminds us that we must enter into prayer humbly, acknowledging that we are finite and limited beings in contrast to the glorious and omnipotent Creator of the universe.

In her essay "An Expedition to the Pole," Annie Dillard wonders if we deliberately close our eyes to God's glory and power. If we truly grasped the immensity of God's strength, she suggests, we would forgo our Sunday best, wear life preservers to church, and lash ourselves to the pews![5] Perhaps we cannot bear the thought that the hand of God, which can turn deserts into verdant plains and rushing rivers, which can crumple mountains like paper, might reach out and touch us. Yet conversely this is also our fervent hope in prayer, that whatever we are facing is as dust before God's limitless power.

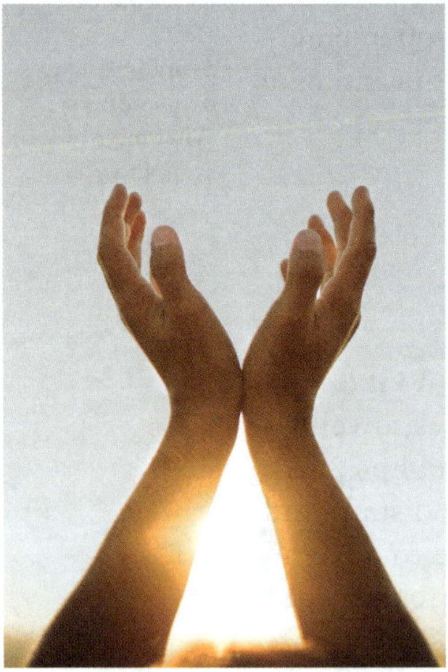

4For your love is better than life;
my lips shall ever praise you!

5I will bless you as long as I live;
I will lift up my hands, calling
on your name.

Praise is the current that carries all our prayer forward to God's throne. Our praises rise like incense to mingle with the eternal chorus of the heavenly hosts singing "Holy, holy, holy" before the throne of God (Rev 4:8). This is what we are ultimately seeking, not just in prayer but in every action of our lives.

We are reminded in this psalm that we pray with our entire selves, not just our minds. As Gregory of Nyssa, one of the early fathers of the church, pointed out, "His divinity is such that it cannot be adequately manifested through verbal signs."[6] No matter how beautiful the words on our lips or how exquisite the music they are set to, expressing all we wish to about God requires even more. It demands our entire being. In one of the psalm-like poems in his *Book of Hours*, Rainer Maria Rilke describes each prayer as a step on a journey, the entire body leaning toward God as a pilgrim might lean into the wind.[7] We go toward God with our breath and our bodies, with our entire lives.

Does praising God come to you naturally? Do you think of praise as its own kind of prayer or as infusing all of your prayers?

In these two verses, the psalmist offers us advice on how to approach prayer with our whole selves—in what we say and in how we hold ourselves when we say it. While we might think of kneeling as the classical posture of prayer, early Christian traditions took the psalmist's advice: stand with arms outstretched, they recommended, your eyes uplifted. Carry in your body the very image of your soul's stance in prayer—looking to God to see his strength and glory, imploring God to come to your rescue, opening arms to receive what God might offer you. St. Dominic's traditional nine ways of prayer include advice on postures for particular types of prayer. Bow, for example, to recall our humility before God; genuflect to express our awe of the Lord God; sit with a spiritual book to be in conversation with God's

What is your favorite prayer posture? How are you most comfortable or most alert? Where do you prefer to pray?

Try the three ways of holding your hands, according to Dominic: hands before you as if reading from a book; hands clasped together; hands raised as a priest does at liturgy. How does changing your prayer posture change your prayer experience?

word. Even walking can be considered a prayer posture![8] We are all on a journey toward God, in praise and posture.

6My soul shall be sated as with choice food,
with joyous lips my mouth shall praise you!

Our prayer might rise like incense to heaven, but God's word returns to fill us completely. We ought not to confuse detachment in prayer (our willingness to accept God's will) with God's indifference toward us. The psalmist reminds us that God desires not only to meet our basic needs but also to lavish us with gifts so that we might never hunger for anything else.

Another translation of this verse uses "exultant" rather than "joyous" to describe the psalmist's response to God's loving generosity (Grail Psalter). "Exult" derives from the Latin word meaning "to leap up." Prayer brings us more than happiness, moves us even beyond joy. In prayer our hearts and minds, our bodies and souls, "leap up" to acknowledge what God has done for us. We look to God in prayer that we, too, might be radiant with joy (Ps 34:6).

Can you recall a time when God answered your prayer much more lavishly than you expected?

7I think of you upon my bed,
I remember you through the watches of the night

It is traditional to pray before we sleep, asking for God's care through the night or murmuring prayers for the safety of family and friends as we drift off. But nighttime is also a time to keep vigil. It is a time when we are particularly awake to the forces that stir in the darkness and equally aware of where our true safety lies.

Prayer in the middle of the night has other advantages. As David Fleming, SJ, suggests in his commentary on the *Spiritual Exercises* of St. Ignatius of Loyola, after a period of sleep both mind and body are quiet, which eases our way into prayer.[9] We learn in these quiet hours what contemplative prayer can be, what it means to rest in God.

What time is most conducive to meditative prayer for you? Do you find your body and mind to be quiet in the middle of the night?

8You indeed are my savior,
and in the shadow of your wings I shout for joy.
9My soul clings fast to you;
your right hand upholds me.

We are not always ready to shout for joy. At times it can feel as if our prayers have gone unanswered or even unheard. What then? In a description of her visions, medieval mystic Julian of Norwich noted that Jesus did not say we will not be tempest-tossed or disturbed. Instead, he promised that we will not be overcome.[10] Likewise the psalms promise us that we will never be alone in our prayer, no matter what we are experiencing.

Reflect back on a time when God was clearly accompanying you. What image would you use to describe what God's presence felt like at that time in your life?

We cling to God, and God clings to us. The parallelism of this verse underscores God's promise of accompaniment. God stays so close to us that we are completely enfolded, as a mother hen protects her chicks under her wings, or as a cloak wraps us in its warmth. As Julian of Norwich wrote, we are clothed in God.[11] Enveloped in his love, God will never let us go.

Praying the Word / Sacred Reading

Jewish biblical scholar André Chouraqui said that the psalms are more than words on a page, for they were first written in the lives and blood of the people of Israel.[12] *It is as necessary to live the psalms as it is to read them. Perhaps the best way to understand what the psalms have to teach us about prayer is to pray them with all our strength and all our soul, allowing our voices to be joined with the chorus that has sung these prayers for thousands of years.*

Pray the following selection from Psalm 27 (vv. 1-8), reading it aloud if possible, even singing it if you know a simple musical setting. When has the Lord been your light and salvation? When has God been a refuge? When have you lived this prayer?

The Lord is my light and my salvation;
whom should I fear?
The Lord is my life's refuge;
of whom should I be afraid?

When evildoers come at me
  to devour my flesh,
These my enemies and foes
  themselves stumble and fall.
Though an army encamp against me,
  my heart does not fear;
Though war be waged against me,
  even then do I trust.

One thing I ask of the LORD;
  this I seek:
To dwell in the LORD's house
  all the days of my life,
To gaze on the LORD's beauty,
  to visit his temple.
For God will hide me in his shelter
  in time of trouble,
He will conceal me in the cover of his tent;
  and set me high upon a rock.
Even now my head is held high
  above my enemies on every side!
I will offer in his tent
  sacrifices with shouts of joy;
  I will sing and chant praise
    to the LORD.

Hear my voice, LORD, when
    I call;
  have mercy on me and
    answer me.
"Come," says my heart,
    "seek his face";
  your face, LORD, do I seek!

Living the Word

Consider finding new ways to weave the psalms into your daily prayer. Try one or more of the following:

- *Rewrite a psalm using words and images that speak to you. For example, you might try Psalm 147, which speaks of snow like wool and frost like ashes.*
- *Find a psalm that speaks particularly to your current situation, whatever that might be. Overflowing with joy? Try Psalm 150. Grieving? The psalmist grieves with you (Psalm 42). Feeling abandoned? Pray Psalm 22 (Jesus' own choice as he died on the cross), or seek the comfort of Psalm 129. In need of mercy? Psalm 51 begs God for a clean heart and a steadfast spirit. Whatever psalm you choose, pray through it slowly, stopping when a line speaks to your heart. Return to it once each day.*
- *Commit Psalm 117—the shortest psalm—to memory. If you benefit from this, you might consider memorizing other, longer psalms.*

Praise the LORD, all you nations!
  Extol him, all you peoples!
His mercy for us is strong;
  the faithfulness of the LORD is forever.
Hallelujah!

Pray without Ceasing

Begin in quiet, asking for God's direction and wisdom as you prayerfully read this passage from Paul's First Letter to the Thessalonians.

1 Thessalonians 5:14-19

[14]We urge you, brothers, admonish the idle, cheer the faint-
hearted, support the weak, be patient with all. [15]See that no
one returns evil for evil; rather, always seek what is good
[both] for each other and for all. [16]Rejoice always. [17]Pray
without ceasing. [18]In all circumstances give thanks, for this
is the will of God for you in Christ Jesus. [19]Do not quench
the Spirit.

Following a few moments of reflection on Paul's words, consider the background information provided below in Setting the Scene.

Setting the Scene

The letters Paul wrote to early Christian communities are a rich source of advice, even for us today. St. Paul was an educated, Greek-speaking Jew born in Tarsus, an important trading city, who around 34 CE experienced a life-shattering encounter with the risen Christ on the road to Damascus. After this transformative encounter, Paul traveled extensively around the Mediterranean basin, proclaiming the Gospel from Antioch to Rome and perhaps even as far afield as Spain. He helped to found a number of Christian communities and supported the nascent Christian movement with his preaching and letters as it spread from Jerusalem throughout the Roman Empire.

In the first century CE, as it is now, Thessalonica was a major port city on the Mediterranean. It was a vibrant trade hub with routes leading east to Rome and west to Byzantium, as well as south toward Corinth and Athens. As was often the case, Paul preached there, established a small community of believers, and then moved on to preach elsewhere. As time passed, Paul's associate Timothy reported to Paul that the community in Thessalonica needed some guidance and encouragement. This report was the catalyst for Paul's letter to the Thessalonians, likely written from Corinth in 50 CE. This is the earliest of the Pauline letters that we have, and scholars believe it to be the first of the New Testament books to be written, pre-dating the gospels.

First Thessalonians is a personal letter, written to console and strengthen the faith of cherished friends, and it incorporates a common topic in Paul's letters: prayer. The passage we will focus on comes from very nearly the end of the letter and is an example of what Pauline scholar Calvin Roetzel dubs "shotgun paraenesis,"[1] a pithy list of advice that, while broadly applicable, was shaped with the struggles of a particular community in mind. Timothy had found the Thessalonians dispirited, their expectations of the imminent return of Jesus unmet. Paul's advice reminded them to care for each other and sought to ground them in the here and now, laying out the expectations of daily life within a Christian community. This daily life included prayer.

Paul was single-minded, devoted to preaching what had been handed on to him: that Jesus Christ was crucified, died, and had risen from the dead for the salvation of the world. He wrote not only to support individual believers in their lives of faith but also to encourage the growing web of Christian communities extending from Jerusalem to Rome and beyond. His advice on living as Christians is no less helpful to us—and no less challenging—than it was to the Thessalonians and other young communities of faith.

The passage from 1 Thessalonians will now be explored a verse at a time. The commentary will help you deepen your understanding of the passage. Continue to use the questions in the margins for personal reflection or group discussion.

Understanding the Scene Itself

14We urge you, brothers, admonish the idle, cheer the fainthearted, support the weak, be patient with all.

In the fourth century CE, a number of men and women withdrew to the Egyptian desert to pray. Many people journeyed on foot to ask these Desert Fathers and Mothers for advice about prayer. Some of that advice has come down to us in a collection called *Sayings of the Fathers* (sayings of Mothers are included as well!). In it we find the story of Abba Poemen—a shepherd who is thought to have been the leader of one of the small communities in the desert. A visitor wondered how Poemen responded when he found one of the brother monks sleeping through prayers in church. Did he prod him awake and reprimand him? No, replied Poemen: "I put his head on my knee and let him rest."[2]

Who might you seek out to ask advice about prayer?

Paul prefaces his advice about prayer with a reminder of our responsibility to care for each other. Like Poemen, he doesn't scold the Thessalonians but stresses the positive steps Christians can take to support each other. We do not undertake our journey of faith alone—at any point we may be the fainthearted, the weak, the one in need of patience or a place to rest our heads when we simply cannot find the wherewithal to pray.

How can you support others in your community in their prayer? What support might you need?

15See that no one returns evil for evil; rather, always seek what is good [both] for each other and for all.

What is the good we seek? The simple answer is what we heard in Psalm 63: we seek God, who is the ultimate good. Here Paul gives us an invitation to reflect on how we—in the specific time and place we find ourselves—ought to live. Paul wants us to consider the shape of our Christian lives as individuals and as communities, in particular what we owe each other as sons and daughters of the living God.

Prayer—our inner relationship with God—can help us recognize what is good and what is evil. In his *Spiritual Exercises*, St. Ignatius of Loyola offers some guidelines (twenty-two of them!) for prayerfully discerning the good. In her book *Inner Compass*, Margaret Silf distills St. Ignatius' list down to its essential core: look for where you find spiritual consolation. Seek those moments where your heart is beating in harmony with God, giving you an abiding sense of peace, even when circumstances themselves may be troubled or distressing.[3]

[16]**Rejoice always.**

Where is joy in your life right now? Can you see God's hand in it? Don't rule out the small joys: the comfort of a hot cup of tea after a wet walk home from the bus stop, or a quick call from a friend.

Joy is the surest sign of the presence of God, wrote nineteenth-century French novelist Léon Bloy.[4] When we are on the lookout for joy, we are on the lookout for God. When our hearts lift in exultation, no matter where we are, we have encountered God. And if God is always present, then how can we do anything except rejoice always?

Scholars suggest Paul intended this triplet of reminders—to unfailingly rejoice, to pray, and to give thanks—to hearten the discouraged Thessalonians, to give them hope. We can read his words as they did, not as an impossible exercise or as a demand to be irrational optimists in the face of real difficulties, but as a reminder to hope in God who is always with us, always offering us a reason to rejoice and to give thanks. We are, as the prophet Zechariah said of the Israelites, prisoners of hope, safe within God, our ever-present fortress (Zech 9:12).

[17]**Pray without ceasing.**

From the earliest days of Christianity, Paul's injunction to "pray always" has had a profound effect on how we live, shaping our prayer lives both as individuals and as faith communities. The Catholic Church prays the Liturgy of the Hours (sometimes called the Divine Office) all around the clock, from Morning Prayer to Night Prayer, including an Office of Readings which can be prayed as a vigil in the middle of the night.

Admittedly, Paul's injunction can feel overwhelming. How can we pray all the time while also tending to the needs of everyday life? The laundry needs doing, children must be watched over, someone must make dinner and do the dishes. St. Teresa of Avila, a sixteenth-century Carmelite nun and one of the thirty-six Doctors of the Church, wrote extensively on the spiritual life and understood this dichotomy well. Her very practical advice to her sisters in the convent can sustain us too: "Understand that even in the kitchen, the Lord walks amid the cookpots helping you in both work and prayer."[5] Her advice is a reminder that prayer is a two-way street: God is always with us, always praying with and in us. We don't have a "regular" life aside from our prayer life; they are one.

What pulls you away from prayer? What reminds you to pray?

The Christian tradition draws a deep connection between breathing and prayer. St. Anthony advised his monks to "breathe Christ at all times."[6] His contemporary St. Gregory of Nazianzus also used the image of the ever-present tempo of our breath to vividly underscore our call to pray at all times: "We must remember God more often than we draw breath."[7] Paul's advice can inspire us to pray as we

breathe—naturally, whether we are consciously thinking of it or not.

[18]In all circumstances give thanks, for this is the will of God for you in Christ Jesus.

What types of prayer do you say least often? Why do you think that is?

When we pray unceasingly, what should we pray for? The four traditional types of prayer are supplication, adoration, contrition, and thanksgiving. We pray to ask God for what we need. We pray to praise the all-powerful, ever-living God. We pray to express our sorrow for having missed the mark in our daily lives and to ask for God's mercy. But of all these, Paul suggests, prayers of gratitude have a special place. St. Ambrose, a fourth-century theologian, composer, and archbishop of Milan, agreed, "No duty is more urgent than that of returning thanks."[8]

Gratitude is a grace, an unmerited gift from God. One of the old prefaces to the eucharistic prayer expresses it this way: "[O]ur desire to thank you is itself your gift."[9] The word "Eucharist" itself derives from the Greek word for "grateful"—*eucharistos*. In *Sacrosanctum Concilium* (Constitution on the Sacred Liturgy), the Second Vatican Council called the Eucharist both the "summit" and the "font" of our Christian lives.[10] In our eucharistic celebrations, we gather to both pour forth our gratitude for what has been done for us and drink from that well of grace. We leave ever more on fire for the Gospel, ever more grateful.

To be grateful in prayer is to be humble, to acknowledge that all we have, all we desire, all we are, and all we will be comes from God alone. The *Catechism of the Catholic Church* thus reminds us that humility is the foundation of prayer.[11] Abba Isaac, one of the Desert Fathers, recommended the repetition of a single psalm verse to everyone who wanted to pray without ceasing: "God, come to my assistance. Lord, make haste to help me" (Ps 70:2). He suggested that the recitation of this particular verse helps us acknowledge our humble need for God's help in whatever we do.[12] This short prayer—or another of our choosing—can also help us do as St. Hildegarde of Bingen recommended: avoid wordiness in our prayer![13]

Is there a specific prayer or verse from a psalm that you reach for in times of need?

Jesus also recommended keeping prayer simple (Matt 6:7-8). Why do you think Jesus taught this, and what does it mean for your prayer life?

[19]Do not quench the Spirit.

Even as our desire for prayer is a gift from God, difficulties in prayer will arise. We can fail to find the words—or the time—for prayer. We may weary of prayer or find it dry and unfulfilling. We can become distracted, tempted away by the bustle of the world around us. We may become discouraged when our prayers seem to go unanswered.

Amma Syncletica, one of the fourth-century Desert Mothers, warned of the weariness of soul that can suck the life out of our prayer, much like the heat and humidity of a summer's afternoon can drain us of energy. She recommended praying the psalms as the cure for this apathy. The psalms, as the very word of God, are alive. They can breathe life into our prayer when it feels wilted or dry in ways that other prayers cannot.[14]

Prayer can be particularly difficult when we are distracted. It can be tempting to watch for distractions so they can each be rooted out, but when we are attentive to the disturbances, we are not attentive to the Lord. The anonymous author of the *Cloud of Unknowing* advised beginners in prayer to try looking "over the shoulders" of the distractions in order to see what is hidden beyond: God.[15]

It is part of the humility we must bring to our lives of faith to recognize that we will inevitably struggle with prayer. Amma Syncletica put it tartly: "Just as one cannot build a ship without nails, it is impossible to be saved without humility."[16] We can humbly seek help in our floundering from saints and spiritual writers, from soul friends and spiritual directors, all of whom have at one time or another struggled in their own prayer lives.

Above all, it may help to recall that even when we can't find the words or the will to pray, the Spirit still wordlessly prays within us. Paul reassured the Romans, "In the same way, the Spirit too comes to the aid of our weakness; for we do not know how to pray as we ought, but the Spirit itself intercedes with inexpressible groanings" (Rom 8:26). Like the very breath within us, the Spirit is always at work.

What are your biggest challenges in prayer? What has helped you deal with them?

Praying the Word / Sacred Reading

St. Augustine was a convert to Christianity and eventually the bishop of Hippo (in modern day Algeria). Around 410 CE, Proba, a widow of a prominent Roman citizen, began a small Christian community of women in what is now Tunisia on the African coast. She wrote to Augustine, whose teachings on prayer were highly regarded, to ask his advice. St. Augustine advised her to follow the practice of the early Christian hermits and resort to frequent, short prayers. Prayer should consist more of "sighs and groanings" than of words. Prayer is essentially letting the Holy Spirit pray in us.[17]

Pray this prayer to the Holy Spirit that is widely attributed to St. Augustine. Imagine the Spirit breathing in you, praying without words and without ceasing.

Breathe in me, O Holy Spirit,
that my thoughts may all be holy.
Act in me, O Holy Spirit,
that my work, too, may be holy.
Draw my heart, O Holy Spirit,
that I love but what is holy.

Strengthen me, O Holy Spirit,
to defend all that is holy.
Guard me, then, O Holy Spirit,
that I always may be holy.

Living the Word

In his short book The Need and the Blessing of Prayer, *theologian Karl Rahner, SJ, reminded us of the importance of small devotions in our everyday lives, whether saying grace before meals or marking children with the sign of the cross before they go to sleep.*[18] *Consider some ways to build frequent prayer into your daily routine this week. Here are a few ideas:*

- *When we want to be sure we don't forget something, we turn to physical reminders. This has long been true of prayer too. According to legend, St. Anthony the Great kept track of his prayers by tying knots in a rope. (The devil kept untying the knots to distract him until St. Anthony had a vision of Mary, the Mother of God, showing him how to tie cross-shaped knots that the devil could not touch.) A rosary tucked into a pocket or purse can serve as a reminder to pray throughout our day. Try saying a decade of the rosary—one Our Father and ten Hail Marys—when you take a break during your day, perhaps at midmorning, midday, and midafternoon.*
- *Seek out joy and thereby God in your day. Don't overlook the small daily joys. Founder*

of the Catholic Worker Movement and candidate for sainthood Dorothy Day found the delight of her morning cup of coffee to be a small moment of encounter with God.[19] *Jot down the joys of each day. Pray gratefully to God in gratitude for these gifts of divine presence.*

- *As St. Augustine advised Proba, choose a short prayer that you can "hurl at the heavens" quickly and easily when you want to call on God. It can be a verse from a psalm or a short traditional prayer such as the Jesus Prayer: "Lord Jesus Christ, Son of the living God, have mercy on me, a sinner."*
- *Poet and composer Leonard Cohen wrote dozens of verses when he was writing his song "Hallelujah" as a way to grapple with the many meanings he heard in the word.*[20] *Was it holy, broken, cold, blazing with light? At the very end of the song, Cohen confesses that in the end he'll stand before the Lord with nothing but the word "Hallelujah" on his lips. Try to respond in prayer to all the events of this week with that one word—alleluia, praise the Lord. Commit to humming it in the ordinary, spitting it through clenched teeth when you are frustrated, crying it aloud in awe at the sunset, howling it in grief at all that is broken in our world. At all times, alleluia. Praise the Lord.*

Teach Us to Pray

Begin in quiet reflection as you ask God to be with you in your prayer and study. Then read this passage from Luke's gospel about prayer.

Luke 11:1-10

1 He was praying in a certain place, and when he had finished, one
of his disciples said to him, "Lord, teach us to pray just as John
taught his disciples." 2 He said to them, "When you pray, say:

Father, hallowed be your name,
your kingdom come.
3 Give us each day our daily bread
4 and forgive us our sins
for we ourselves forgive everyone in debt to us,
and do not subject us to the final test."

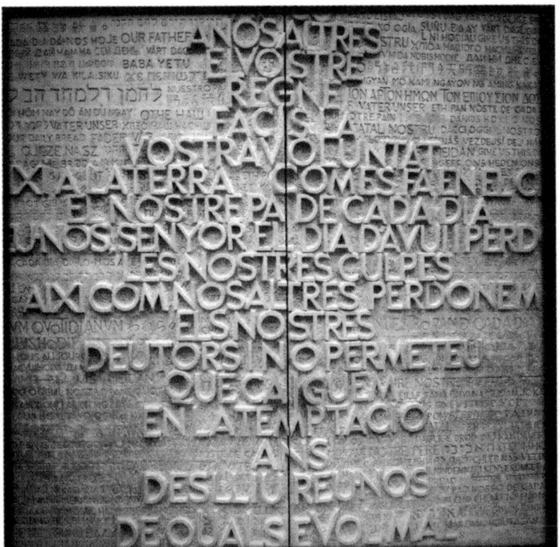

The Our Father on the doors of the Sagrada Familia Basilica in Barcelona.

**5And he said to them, "Suppose one of you has
a friend to whom he goes at midnight and says,
'Friend, lend me three loaves of bread, 6for a
friend of mine has arrived at my house from a
journey and I have nothing to offer him,' 7and
he says in reply from within, 'Do not bother me;
the door has already been locked and my chil-
dren and I are already in bed. I cannot get up to
give you anything.' 8I tell you, if he does not get
up to give him the loaves because of their friend-
ship, he will get up to give him whatever he
needs because of his persistence.**

**9"And I tell you, ask and you will receive; seek
and you will find; knock and the door will be
opened to you. 10For everyone who asks, re-
ceives; and the one who seeks, finds; and to the
one who knocks, the door will be opened."**

Following a few moments of quiet reflection, consider the background information provided below in Setting the Scene. Continue using the questions in the margins for personal reflection or group discussion.

Setting the Scene

The authorship of the Third Gospel is traditionally attributed to Luke of Antioch, a companion of St. Paul and a physician (Col 4:14). Likely written in the 80s CE (decades after Paul's first letter to the Thessalonians), Luke's gospel was oriented toward Christians who, while living in the hope of Christ's second coming, were in need of practical advice regarding the daily living-out

Read and reflect on the other two parables about prayer in Luke's gospel (18:1-8 and 18:9-14). What do you learn about prayer? Do you find anything difficult or problematic?

Read the story of Martha and Mary (Luke 10:38-42). Can you relate to this tension between the desire for prayer and the need for action? Which are you more drawn to? How do you handle this tension in your life?

of their faith. So it is not surprising that this gospel includes so much guidance about prayer.

Luke's version of the Our Father (see also Matt 6:9-13) and the parable of the persistent neighbor (one of three Lukan parables on prayer; see also Luke 18:1-14) appear early in Luke's account of Jesus' journey to Jerusalem. The verses that immediately precede this excerpt recount the story of Martha and Mary (10:38-42). In this familiar story, Luke explores the tension between our desire to sit with the Lord, listening attentively, and the demands and tasks of daily life. How should we integrate prayer with our necessary activities?

As we read this excerpt from Luke's gospel, we will keep this and other questions about prayer in mind. Clearly, even the disciples of Jesus had questions. The passage begins with their request that Jesus teach them to pray.

> *Luke 11:1-10 will now be explored a few verses at a time to deepen your understanding of the passage. Spend time with the text and the questions along the way.*

Understanding the Scene Itself

[1]He was praying in a certain place, and when he had finished, one of his disciples said to him, "Lord, teach us to pray just as John taught his disciples."

The disciples are directly asking Jesus how to reach out to God. Like the psalmists, they desire to find God in prayer: "'Come,' says my heart, 'seek his face'" (Ps 27:8). Again and again they have seen Jesus pray. Indeed, Luke's gospel recounts seven times Jesus goes off to pray—in deserted places, on mountain tops, and finally, in a garden (3:21; 5:16; 6:12; 9:18, 28; 11:1; 22:41).

Like the disciples, we too want clear instructions on how to pray. We want to know not only how to pray but how to pray *like Jesus*—how to be in close communion with God. In response to the disciples' pleas—and, tacitly, ours—Jesus is brief and direct. He offers no esoteric language; he has nothing to say about what gestures to make, what clothes to wear, or when or where to pray. In the course of a few dozen words, he tells us all we need to know about how to pray.

Like Naaman, who was puzzled by the prophet Elisha's straightforward recommendation to bathe in the river Jordan to cure his leprosy (2 Kgs 5:10-14), we too might be surprised by Jesus' succinct and simple advice on prayer. Evagrius, one of the Desert Fathers, underscored this advice. Evagrius advised against complex prayer regimens lest we wear ourselves out before we have gone very far. Instead, he said, we should start gently and slowly stretch ourselves.[1] It's not ultimately about the heights we reach in prayer;

What would you want to ask Jesus about prayer? How do you think he might answer?

what God desires most is our heartfelt intention to seek him in prayer.

[2]He said to them, "When you pray, say:

Father, hallowed be your name,
your kingdom come.

While we might not be surprised that Jesus would address God with the intimate title *Father*, it might surprise us that this is how Jesus tells us to begin our prayers. Jesus is reminding us that we should come to prayer aware that we are God's beloved children. We are calling on a God who is not distant and forbidding but who is our source of life and who, like a good parent, is a tenderly attentive caregiver. Jesus tells us we are praying to a God who cherishes us and whom we love.

Can you imagine having an informal conversation with God, as with a friend? What are the benefits of this kind of prayer?

St. Teresa of Avila advised those seeking to deepen their prayer life to draw on this loving relationship. The most important thing, she said, was not to think much but to love much. Teresa counseled beginners to avoid bursting into a torrent of words. Instead, she encouraged them to engage in friendly conversation with our Lord and then gradually let the words fall away, relaxing and delighting in the silence like two friends who have known each other for a long time or like a parent and child who have spent a great deal of time together.[2] Teresa's advice reminds us that we can simply enjoy God's presence.

In this verse, we are once again reminded that humility is the foundation of prayer. We ought not, as an anonymous Carthusian monk so bluntly put it, get puffed up like frogs when we pray.[3] Even as we call God "Father," Jesus reminds us to recognize God's power and glory, the holiness of his very name. We yearn not for the riches of this world but for the kingdom that is promised.

[3]Give us each day our daily bread

In Luke's gospel, bread is more than literal food for the body; it is whatever sustains our lives. Prayer sustains our souls much as bread sustains our bodies. The *Didache*, a first-century manual for Christians, advised praying the Our Father three times a day.[4] Two thousand years later, the church continues to recommend this practice, with the Our Father prayed at Morning Prayer, Evening Prayer, and at Mass. Even if we do not keep the Hours or cannot go to Mass daily, we can still pray Jesus' words three times a day, seeking what feeds us most.

What do you ask God for each day? What do you need?

Jesus tells us to prayerfully ask for what we need today, to focus our concerns on the here and now rather than worrying about the future. We are urged to ask for what we need, which implicitly requires us to distinguish our needs from our wants. We are also encouraged to accept what we are given, or as St. Catherine of Siena put it, to "sail with the wind heaven sends us."[5]

4and forgive us our sins
for we ourselves forgive everyone in debt
to us,
and do not subject us to the final test."

God certainly knows our desire for mercy, but here again we are urged to recognize this need for ourselves. We are sinners, redeemed by Christ's sacrifice on the cross, but sinners nonetheless.

Do you pray for the "troublesome," for those that annoy you or have hurt you? If not, what might be holding you back?

Next we are encouraged to bring a generous spirit to our prayer. As Christ forgives, so should we forgive. Jesus prompts us to set aside our grudges and open wide our hearts. One of the regular intercessions in the Liturgy of the Hours asks forgiveness for the times we fail to see and reverence Christ in the "troublesome."[6] As difficult as it can be at times to pray for those who have troubled us, we must recognize the merciful Christ in ourselves as well as the Christ in each other.

The Our Father as we typically pray it ends "and lead us not into temptation, but deliver us from evil." Why would God tempt us? In a commentary on this gospel, Robert J. Karris, OFM, notes that for Luke, temptations do not build character. They are not an education by ordeal but something to be avoided at all costs. He suggests that the prayer here is for God to keep our feet on the path, to keep us from falling away.[7]

[5]And he said to them, "Suppose one of you has
a friend to whom he goes at midnight and says,
'Friend, lend me three loaves of bread, [6]for a
friend of mine has arrived at my house from a
journey and I have nothing to offer him,' [7]and
he says in reply from within, 'Do not bother me;
the door has already been locked and my chil-
dren and I are already in bed. I cannot get up to
give you anything.' [8]I tell you, if he does not get
up to give him the loaves because of their friend-
ship, he will get up to give him whatever he
needs because of his persistence.

We are encouraged in this parable to be bold and audacious in prayer. The Greek word translated in verse 8 as "persistence" (*anaideia*) might also be rendered as "shamelessness." Jesus wants us to know that we shouldn't hesitate to go to God for whatever we require, no matter how unreasonable it might seem. We can never ask too much of God, nor can we ask too little. In his *Letters to Malcolm: Chiefly on Prayer*, C. S. Lewis cautioned against being too high-minded in prayer. We ought not to be put off from small prayers by "a sense of our own dignity rather than God's."[8]

To dance well, choreographer Merce Cunningham once said, "you have to love the daily working."[9] The repetitive exercises and the stretching of muscles to their limits allow the ethereal and effortless leaps of a dancer on stage. This is good advice for prayer as well. We need to love our persistent routine of prayer as much as we cherish joyously unbidden moments of communion with the divine. We need to be faithful to prayer in our daily lives.

What are your daily prayer habits? What helps you stay committed to prayer?

Still, amid our busy lives, it can be difficult to find time to be "unproductive" in prayer. But such nonproductiveness is essential. "[B]eing useless and silent in the presence of our God belongs to the core of all prayer," wrote Henri Nouwen.[10] Can we practice simply letting God look at us—saying nothing, doing nothing, simply coming to prayer each and every day?

9"And I tell you, ask and you will receive; seek and you will find; knock and the door will be opened to you. 10For everyone who asks, receives; and the one who seeks, finds; and to the one who knocks, the door will be opened.

One translation of Psalm 116 reads, "Because he bends down to listen, / I will pray as long as I have breath!" (v. 2, *New Living Translation*).[11] Jesus encourages us to keep praying, stating clearly that God is listening and will respond. This is a heartening piece of advice.

It can be difficult to keep praying when our prayers seem to go unanswered, if not unheard. Have we not been persistent enough if we don't get what we ask for? Or have we mistaken a want for a need? It can be tempting to think that if we prayed harder, or more often, or better, God would give us what we have asked for. Karl Rahner, SJ, reminds us that our prayers of petition are a pledge of our faith in God, who burns like fire in the darkness of the world.[12] They are our hope for life amid our constant dying and a vow of love that seeks no reward. We ought never to give up.

It remains that the kingdom has not yet come, and evil with all of its attendant chaos is still afoot in the world. But Jesus assures us we are never unheard or abandoned, even when we are in desperate straits and what we are praying for seems to go unfulfilled. Prayer, in that it is part of our relationship with a transcendent and ultimately indescribable God, can never be reduced to a predictable transaction. Elements of mystery, and so confusion, will always remain, for our ways are not God's ways (Isa 55:8). Yet there is one thing we know for certain: the encounter with the divine is itself the ultimate answer to any prayer.

What new thoughts or ideas do you have about prayer? How might your prayer habits or methods change going forward?

Praying the Word / Sacred Reading

In an appendix to his Spiritual Exercises, *St. Ignatius of Loyola outlined three simple ways to pray meditatively. The third of these methods relies on the rhythm of the breath to pace a meditative recitation of a common prayer. Ignatius used the example of the Our Father to illustrate his method. With each breath, he instructed, say one word of the prayer, letting the meaning of that word flood your mind.*[13] *For example, pray "Our" and reflect on how we are cherished by God, how we are his people and he our God. On the next breath, continue with the next word, "Father," and so on, until the prayer is complete. Pray the Our Father—or another favorite prayer—to the rhythm of your breath.*

Living the Word

- *The great bronze doors of Antoni Gaudí's magnificent basilica, Sagrada Família in Barcelona, are inscribed with the words of the Our Father in fifty different languages, including Arabic, Wolof, and Gaudí's native tongue, Catalan. The doors to this place of prayer remind us that these words are also a door into prayer for people of all nations. If you know the Our Father in another language, pray with it this week. What words speak most to your heart in each translation?*
- *Just as the Spirit prays in us with wordless groanings (Rom 8:26), music can deepen our experience of prayer. Seek out and listen to a recording of the Our Father (many can be found with an internet search). Try Renaissance composer Jacob Handl's choral arrangement in Latin or the lively Soweto*

Gospel Choir's recording of the Our Father in Swahili—"Baba Yetu." Australian composer Lisa Gerrard and Irish composer Patrick Cassidy have set the Aramaic translation to a haunting chant in "Abwoon (Our Father)," giving us an echo of Jesus' words in his own language.

- *As the early Christians did, pray the Our Father three times a day this week.*
- *In the Our Father, we pray to forgive as we wish to be forgiven. In her book* A Stone for a Pillow, *Madeleine L'Engle suggests it is "salutary to bless six people [you] don't much like every morning before breakfast."*[14] *Who might you forgive—and even bless—today when you pray?*
- *We pray for the kingdom of God to come. What can we do to help make the kingdom present to those around us? Commit to aiding someone in your community this week, whether it is buying food for the local food bank or bringing dinner to a neighbor overwhelmed by caring for children or an ill family member. In these actions of love, your prayer and work are united.*

Notes

Prologue

1. Kieran Kavanaugh, *John of the Cross: Selected Writings* (New York: Paulist Press, 1987), 280.

Thirsting for God

1. CCC 2596.
2. Thomas Merton, *Praying the Psalms* (Collegeville, MN: Liturgical Press, 1956), 11.
3. CCC 2697.
4. Augustine of Hippo, *Tractate 15 (John 4:1-42)*, https://www.newadvent.org/fathers/1701015.htm.
5. Annie Dillard, *Teaching a Stone to Talk: Expeditions and Encounters* (New York: Harper Perennial, 2013), 52.
6. Gregory of Nyssa, quoted in *Galatians, Ephesians, Philippians: Ancient Christian Commentary on Scripture*, ed. Mark J. Edwards (Downers Grove, IL: InterVarsity Press, 2005), 242.
7. Rainer Maria Rilke, *Rilke's Book of Hours: Love Poems to God*, trans. Anita Barrows and Joanna Macy (New York: Riverhead Books, 2005), 84.
8. S. Chris Broslavick, "St. Dominic's Nine Ways of Prayer," https://www.racinedominicans.org/about-us/prayer.cfm.
9. David L. Fleming, SJ, *Draw Me into Your Friendship: A Literal Translation and a Contemporary Reading of the Spiritual Exercises* (St. Louis, MO: Institute of Jesuit Sources, 1996), 63–65.
10. Julian of Norwich, *Revelations of Divine Love Recorded by Julian, Anchoress at Norwich*, trans. Grace Warrack (London: Methuen, 1901), 169–70.
11. Julian of Norwich, 10.
12. André Chouraqui, "The Psalms," *Liturgy OCSO* 13 (February 1979): 3–36.

Pray without Ceasing

1. Raymond F. Collins, *Studies on the First Letter to the Thessalonians* (Leuven, Belgium: Leuven University Press, 1984), 25.
2. Benedicta Ward, SLG, *The Sayings of the Desert Fathers: The Alphabetical Collection* (Collegeville, MN: Liturgical Press, 1984), 179–80.
3. Margaret Silf, *Inner Compass* (Chicago: Loyola Press, 1999).
4. Léon Bloy and Barbara Wald, trans., *Letters to His Fiancée* (New York: Sheed & Ward, 1937), 57.
5. Teresa of Avila, *Libro de las fundaciones, Vol. 3* (Madrid: 1916), 35.
6. Gabriel Bunge, OSB, *Earthen Vessels: The Practice of Personal Prayer According to the Patristic Tradition*, trans. Michael J. Miller (San Francisco: Ignatius Press, 2002), 111.
7. CCC 2697.
8. St. Ambrose, *De excessu fratris Satyri [On the Passing of His Brother Satyrus]*, Book I, ch. 44 or https://www.newadvent.org/fathers/34031.htm.
9. Preface for Weekdays IV, 1985 version.
10. *Sacrosanctum Concilium* 10, in Austin Flannery, ed., *Vatican Council II: Constitutions, Decrees, Declarations; The Basic Sixteen Documents* (Collegeville, MN: Liturgical Press, 2014).
11. CCC 2559.
12. John Cassian, *John Cassian: The Conferences*, trans. Boniface Ramsey, OP (New York: Newman Press, 1997), 379.
13. Hugh Feiss, OSB, *Essential Monastic Wisdom* (New York: Harper Collins, 1999), 17.
14. Ward, *Sayings of the Desert Fathers*, 235.
15. William Johnston, ed., *The Cloud of Unknowing and The Book of Privy Counseling* (New York: Image Books, 1973), 88.
16. Ward, *Sayings of the Desert Fathers*, 235.
17. Augustine of Hippo, *Letter 130*, 20, https://www.newadvent.org/fathers/1102130.htm.
18. Karl Rahner, SJ, *The Need and the Blessing of Prayer* (Collegeville, MN: Liturgical Press, 1997), 37–47.
19. Dorothy Day and Robert Ellsberg, eds., *The Duty of Delight: The Diaries of Dorothy Day* (New York: Image, 2007), 243.

20. Leonard Cohen, *Various Positions* (Columbia, 1984).

Teach Us to Pray

1. Evagrius, quoted in *Mark: Ancient Christian Commentary on Scripture*, ed. Thomas Oden and Christopher Hall (Downers Grove, IL: InterVarsity Press, 2005), 179.
2. Ernest Larkin, O Carm, "St. Teresa of Avila Speaks on Mental Prayer," http://carmelnet.org/larkin/larkin087.pdf.
3. A Carthusian, *The Wound of Love* (Herefordshire: Gracewing, 2006), 71.
4. *Didache*, chapter 8, https://www.newadvent.org/fathers/0714.htm.
5. Sigrid Undset, *Catherine of Siena* (San Francisco: Ignatius Press, 2009), 219.
6. *Christian Prayer: The Liturgy of the Hours* (New York: Catholic Book Publishing, 1976), 297.
7. Robert J. Karris, OFM, "The Gospel According to Luke," *The New Jerome Biblical Commentary*, ed. Raymond E. Brown, SS; Joseph A. Fitzmyer, SJ; and Roland E. Murphy, O Carm (Upper Saddle River, NJ: Prentice Hall, 1990), 703.
8. C. S. Lewis, *Letters to Malcolm: Chiefly on Prayer* (New York: Harcourt, 1991), 23.
9. Merce Cunningham, quoted in Susan Rethorst, "Dailiness," *A Choreographic Mind: Autobodygraphical Writings* (Helsinki: Theatre Academy Helsinki, 2012).
10. Henri Nouwen, *Reaching Out: The Three Movements of the Spiritual Life* (New York: Image Books, 1986), 136.
11. *Holy Bible: New Living Translation* (Carol Stream, IL: Tyndale, 2017).
12. Karl Rahner, SJ, *The Need and the Blessing of Prayer* (Collegeville, MN: Liturgical Press, 1997), 59.
13. Louis J. Puhl, SJ, *The Spiritual Exercises of St. Ignatius* (Chicago: Loyola University Press, 1951), 112.
14. Madeleine L'Engle, *A Stone for a Pillow* (Wheaton, IL: Shaw, 2000), 121.